Give

Her Back Her

CROWN

Empowering Women to Rebuild Broken Queens

Author: Lakisha Ginyard Louissaint

Ginyard Publishing
Inspiring the World Through Faith

Scripture taken from the New Century Version®. Copyright © 2005 by Thomas Nelson, Inc. Used by permission.

ISBN: 978-0-9992116-6-3
Publisher: Ginyard Publishing
Website: www.IamLakisha.com
Email Us: ginyardpublishing@gmail.com
Library of Congress Control Number: 2020945939

Previous Books:
Tears of Silence (2013); A Broken Marriage with Hidden Secrets 1 (2015); A Broken Marriage with Hidden Secrets 2: Unfinished Business (2016); A Broken Marriage with Hidden Secrets 3: The Conclusion (2017); **The Novel:** A Broken Marriage with Hidden Secrets (2017)

The Crown

Even when her crown is tilted; straighten it. If it falls;
pick it up, wipe it off, and place it back on her head. If
she feels unworthy; remind her of who she is in Christ,
but whatever you do, don't you dare take it.

#GiveHerBackHerCrown

Introduction

Remember the whisper? It was a game that many of us played. It would start with someone whispering a phrase or a sentence in our ears to pass on to the other, but somewhere along the way, the message was misinterpreted based upon the individual's perception of the message. And by the time it reached the end, it was something totally different.

That brings me to this, where did the message of unified Queens inspiring, encouraging, and building up one another go wrong? The harsh reality is, that our emotions misguided us. The message of unity was misconstrued by our pains and unresolved issues with one another. It was misunderstood by the perception of the whisper that no one else could hear, but her. And in that moment, unity then became division, but now is the time that we as Queens of God reunite again.

His Persistence

God has been so persistent in our lives. He's been persistent in loving us, forgiving us, providing for us, covering us, protecting us, and giving us back our crowns that the world and many other broken Queens have managed to tilt or snatch away through their own pain. But, things can change if we simply learn to love, forgive, cover, and encourage one another just as Christ has done for us.

OUR TRUEST IDENTITY

Is in Who we Really Are;
not in the **illusion** *of*
who we *Hope* will be Accepted!

Prayer: Lord, allow me to find who I authentically am in You, not in who I think will be accepted by others. In Jesus name Amen!

CHAPTER ONE
Understanding Who We Are

Have you ever been so lost that you couldn't seem to find the Queen behind your name? Or better yet, have you lost yourself in the illusion of who you thought would be accepted? Well I have, more times than I can count. Sadly, I was willing to play the role of the most popular character just to fit in because I wasn't confident in who I was in Christ. I lost myself all for the sake of people, until I decided to set out on a journey to find the part of me that had been hiding.

Marianne Williamson once said, *"Our deepest fear is not that we are inadequate. Our deepest fear is that we are powerful beyond measure. It is our light, not our darkness that most frightens us. We ask ourselves, 'Who am I to be brilliant, gorgeous, talented, or fabulous?' Actually, who are you not to be? You are a child of God."*

You see, when we lose our identity in people and things, we become disappointed after we realize that we'll never meet their expectations. And on that journey, to find ourselves, the probability of us tearing down another Queen is very high.

On our journeys to embracing that we are Daughters of a King, our traumas come with attempts to dismantle us before we sit down at our inherited thrones in Christ. When this happens, pride slips in causing us to once again prove that we're okay while we're dying on the inside. Then, we begin seeking validation from people instead of God.

As we do this, our crowns begin to tilt and Queens, you know what comes next? You guessed right; we begin to tilt the crowns of our fellow sisters. But why? Because we really don't know who we are. We have yet to find our true identity in Christ; therefore, causing us to feel inadequate and that in itself makes us feel unworthy.

As I journeyed to find myself, I was reminded of the crowns that I too had tilted. What I would give to have the opportunity to look those Queens in their eyes and be accountable for being immature, prideful, and selfish. But for now, I want to remind you of this:

You are Redeemed, Forgiven, & More than a Conqueror. You are Complete & Lacking Nothing. You are **FREE**, Holy, & Without Blame. You are Chosen.

The things that causes us to fall contrary to who we are, are the traumas that we so desperately wish would go away. It's crazy how our identity gets lost in our pains and traumatic experiences. And rightfully so, when we fall, we seek grace from God; yet many times we refuse to reciprocate that same grace to others.

We must pray to become selfless so that we can extend grace as we help rebuild broken Queens and celebrate them as they grow in Christ and walk in their purpose. And as we celebrate one another, we'll find that there has always been beauty in our pain. We are more alike than we are different, but we can only witness that when we take the time to sit down and have a conversation with another sister that we've had or have unresolved issues with.

If we only understood that our fellow sisters' pain will one day transition into healing, we'll then see that she won't always be angry, frustrated, lost, prideful, or broken. At some point, God will heal her just as He's done for us. If we rush her through the traumatic experiences that she has yet to process or understand, she'll place them all in one box; therefore, causing her to lose herself because she doesn't know where to begin digging because of our impatience with her.

She'll then lose sight of how to compartmentalize the trials she's experienced and will be yet another broken and fallen Queen. She'll fall to drugs, alcohol, promiscuity, gossip or whatever her pain leads her to. Then, she will have inevitably lost focus of who she is in Christ because of being consumed by the embarrassment and shame from what she's been through and the whispers that she hears as she walks in a room.

How do I know? I was she and she too has been you. So, how do we get to a place where Healed Queens Rebuild Broken Queens without diminishing and degrading them? We can first begin by searching within to see that we misinterpreted the seasons in her life and her pain.

SEASONS

Represent the transition from Pain to

Being Healed

Prayer: Lord, give me peace in each season of my life. Allow me to encourage others in their seasons that I don't quite understand. Lord, heal them just as you have done for me. In Jesus name Amen!

CHAPTER TWO
Understanding the Seasons

I've heard it many times before, that if someone isn't growing with you, their season is up in your life. I many times wonder where this saying originated from and why? Did impatience or unresolved issues birth it? (Or) Did our misinterpretation of the Queens pain we've encountered cause us to give up on her prematurely?

When we misinterpret the seasons in someone's life, we miss out on the beautiful message that leads to their healing. So, let me take a moment to explain. During another Queen's winter when the earth is tilted away from the sun, our beloved Queen is in a space of lost hope and she's no longer close to "The Son of God" because the trials in her life have caused her to become distant.

With no support and unconditional love, she weathers a cold lonely winter desperately seeking God's help the best way she knows how. But even then, she's so exposed to the enemy that she feels defeated. Every season in her life brings forth new lessons and no matter their extent, she must find the treasure in her pain and find her stability in Christ by understanding that the wisdom she'll gain is more valuable than how she feels.

During this cold winter, God's love begins to remind her that one day, her pain will transition into healing. So, instead of leaving her stranded in the dark to find her way, we must wrap her in love and patience.

You see, seasons don't leave; they simply transition into the other and if we're not careful, we could possibly cause another Queen to give up when she could be reminded that she's still worthy. Her pruning seasons are designed to cut away bad habits and negative mindsets so that when she springs forth, she'll bloom with new perspectives. New perspectives that leads to freedom, but not just any freedom. Her freedom won't be dependent upon people; it will be dependent upon God and who The Son sets free, is free indeed.

As the winter transitions into spring, God begins to show how He created beauty with the ashes of her broken spirit. **Isaiah 61:3** says, *I will give them a crown to replace their ashes, and oil of gladness to replace their sorrow, and clothes of praise to replace their broken spirit of sadness. Then, they will be called trees planted by the Lord to show His greatness.* (NCV)

That's a beauty that reveals God's unconditional love for her and it can also be a lesson for us. Broken Queens were created by a powerful God that chooses to remold her into who He desires for her to be. That Queens pain transitioned into healing because He didn't give up on her and as she blossoms, we must be willing to water her with kindness, gentleness, patience, and inspiring messages that will fertilize her broken spirit.

And before we know it, that once broken Queens light will begin to shine bright and become a light in someone else's darkness. But how? Because God is birthing new things in her life. (Isaiah 43:18-19) She won't be so quick to fumble in the dark or shiver from the cold because she will be embraced by the warmth of God's love.

But, **IF** she becomes content with her growth in the midst of her healing; tucked away unresolved issues will resurface like a sharks fin in the ocean, but since we're talking about seasons, they'll ride in on the summer heat waves and strong storms revealing her broken heart and the shame that she hoped no one would notice.

In the fall, when life tries to knock her down; her growth will seem slim to none and as the daylight falls back, so will others causing her to experience rejection again like never before. And where there's rejection, the warmth of love is absent.

As her leaves begin to change colors and appear to be dying, her untamed emotions (Attitudes Towards Life) begins to resurface. You know, the anger and frustrations that screams, "Give Up. God Doesn't Love You? It's Pointless To Keep Going!!!"

You know, the emotions that we all experience deemed as "negative energy" that causes many to walk away leaving yet another Broken Queen to die. And as she goes through her pruning season once again, instead of being encouraged, the whispers begin, "How did she get back to this place again?"

Remember, seasons simply transition and even if we walk away, God will still allow her to grow and blossom into the woman that He's purposed her to be. Queens, it's vital that we water her with love in her tough seasons; not belittle, degrade, or hate her. Truthfully, we'd all be a mess if God left us in our dry seasons.

His timing is not our timing and His ways are not our ways, but if we acknowledge Him, He will direct our paths and I feel that God is directing us to rebuild broken Queens in Him; not who we think they should be. One day, they'll be spiritually strong enough to help rebuild others. That's why we must **Stand** in love, **Build** in love, and **Never** Give Up On Her. She's simply another Queen in need of God's unconditional love just as we all are.

She was pruned for
New Perspectives to Grow.

Prayer: Lord, help me to not give up on others in their pruning season. Open my mind to the truth that pruning represents preparation for new things to grow. In Jesus name Amen!

CHAPTER THREE
You Are Enough

We've all experienced how doubt and opinions bring forth insecurities, but I want to remind you once again that you are worthy. As your perspectives shift, you will begin to experience new possibilities that will guide you to your purpose. It's the echoes of our past that try to speak louder than the voice of God. And as it screams, it causes many of us to become so lost in our pain that we project it on to others.

But God didn't look at the mistakes we've made and change His mind about us. He meant every single word of it. That means, that we're able to confidently walk in His promises for our lives. Why? Because we are enough. Queens, we're full of possibilities. It really doesn't matter that our past is full of mistakes and pain. What matters is that young Queens are watching and waiting for us to get back up, dust ourselves off, and walk in our purpose. They don't care about our fall. They care about our recovery. They're watching as we regain our footing and strength to help heal and rebuild another Queen. So, we must drown out the noise and forgive those who hurt us; including ourselves. Then, we must go back and make it right just as we did as little girls. And in doing so, we'll find that our ability to love and forgive made another Queen feel worthy again.

Bouncing back won't be easy; but it'll be worth it. But how? Because we have the ability to pick healthy thoughts (New Perspectives) from the new garden of our minds and no longer rely on the unhealthy thoughts that we were trained to think. The beautiful flowers in our field of new perspectives will cause us to see that argument we had and what someone said about us differently. It will open our minds to new possibilities and an understanding that maybe, just maybe it was a misunderstanding or miscommunication on both parts. It will allow us to remove pride and lift our heads from shame by walking in the fact that we are worthy. Our identity is in Christ who loves us unconditionally; not the pain, the shame, the mistakes, the lies, or the slander. So, we must silence the unhealthy emotions and thoughts that try to control us.

When I was younger, I didn't feel worthy enough to be a leaf on a tree. I didn't feel strong enough to hold on. I figured the wind would knock me to the ground, then I would wither and die. I didn't know that I was enough because I was covered in the shame that made me feel as though I had no value to offer the world. Somewhere along the way, God changed my perspectives and I regained my confidence in Him.

As my eyes began to open, I realized that many young Queens were watching and my unhealthy decisions were molding them. I began to realize the power of my influence. I realized that I had a choice to pass on a baton of poison or grant them access to a new and healthier me filled with new possibilities and new perspectives on life. In order for me to get to that place, God had to renew my mind and my confidence in Him and I now share that with you. Don't get me wrong, I'm still learning and my flesh and fickle emotions sometimes get the best of me, but that's when I have to take a step back, reevaluate my heart, submit to God, and be the example that He has called me to be. If I lower my head in shame because people witnessed my fall, then they will too, but, if I dust myself off, they'll witness my strength and ability to recover and that will lead them to even greater possibilities.

Queens big or small, you are enough. You are worthy. You're not your past or the pain that you've experienced! And you definitely aren't the disfunction that tried to mold you! You have purpose in Christ; therefore, you're worthy enough to help rebuild our beloved broken Queens! So, get back up and recover from your fall and help rebuild other broken Queens.

The goal is to

Build; not break.
Lift; not tear down.

Unite
and not divide.
We Are Powerful Together!

Prayer: Lord, give me words to build those who are broken and to lift those who are torn down. Help me to unite with other Queens as One Body in Christ. In Jesus name Amen!

CHAPTER FOUR
Rebuilding Broken Queens!

We are Queens uniting as one body in Christ. Queens who straighten crowns and not tilt them. We are Queens who understand the importance of reminding other Queens of their worth by loving and accepting them right where they are. Our goal is to Build; not break. Lift; not tear down. Unite; and not divide.

And as we do so God's way, we will be able to rebuild broken Queens that have been torn down by this world's unethical morals, religion, jealousy, gossip, hate, and unforgiveness by standing on the truth.

The truth is, that the enemy desires for us to fight against one another, but *Ephesians 6:12* says it like this, *our fight is not against people on earth but against the rulers and authorities and the powers of this world's darkness, against the spiritual powers of evil in the heavenly world.*

Queens, reconstruction begins when we're able to face the truth that our fellow sisters **_aren't_** our enemies. Therefore, we must be open to having those tough conversations as to why and how that once strong wall of unity was torn down, so that healing can be begin.

Matthew 18:15-17 says, "If your fellow believer sins against you, go and tell him in private what he did wrong. If he listens to you, you have helped that person to be your brother or sister again. But if he refuses to listen, go to him again and take one or two other people with you. 'Every case may be proved by two or three witnesses.' If he refuses to listen to them, tell the church. If he refuses to listen to the church, then treat him like a person who does not believe in God or like a tax collector. (NCV)

We must remember that we are Queens of a King who loves us all unconditionally and we too must love one another with the understanding that we're stronger together. If we continue to walk around spiritually blind fighting one another, we'll lose sight of satan; our true enemy who comes to deceptively encourage us all to remain divided.

But, when we as unified Queens stand firm on a strong foundation in Christ, we'll be able to present patience, kindness, and gentleness to one another. This is where our endurance is built. You know, what we need to help us peacefully stand firm when our fellow broken Queens need to experience God's love through us on their way to becoming whole again.

I guess the question is, are we truly living for God through love, forgiveness, and peace? (Or) Are we working for the enemy who wants to rob us of our purpose through fighting one another, unforgiveness, and division? Our answers sit within and as we take the time to search our hearts, we'll discover if we're a part of the problem or if we're a part of the solution.

There, we will find the issues that will reveal that which causes us to become irritated when another Queen experiences raw emotions that shake us to the core. Her anger, frustration, and moments of exploding may be just the things that taps on our own traumas; therefore, evoking emotions we assumed were dead, but her pain caused it to resurface like an empty bottle floating on water. Queens, her pain simply reveals our impatience, lack of self-control, and inability to stand firm when things get hard for her.

Trust me, rebuilding broken Queens won't go down without a fight. That's why we must stand shoulder to shoulder and back to back in prayer so that we'll see the enemy coming from every angle. We must be diligent in prayer and our times of fasting being sure that the enemy doesn't use us to tilt, knock down, or snatch another Queens crown. We must stand firm in unity and no longer remain as divided and defeated Queens. That Queens season isn't up in our lives; it just transitioned into the other and revealed our impatience with her.

She's simply another face with the same pain that you just ran from. We can't win the race if we avoid the hurdles (Our Issues With One Another). There's just no way around it. Love is the glue that will hold us all together and God's truth is our foundation.

So, as we journey to unite as one in Christ, our younger Queens will be influenced to do the same; therefore, creating a movement of love and healing like never before. Let's Rebuild Queens; not slay them!

Be Careful with the
POWER
of your
INFLUENCE

Prayer: Lord, please forgive me for hindering the growth of those who look up to me because I wasn't mindful of the power of my influence. Help me to pay closer attention to what I say, what I do, and how I act so that it will all reflect You. In Jesus name Amen!

CHAPTER FIVE
The Power of Influence

Influence is something that we all have and if we're not careful, it can be detrimental for the lives of the young Queens quietly watching us. Beatrix Potter once said, *"I hold that a strongly marked personality can influence descendants for generations."*

Queens, that's powerful because, growing up we've all seen things that impacted our lives in both a negative and positive way. The older we got, we realized how powerful its influence was. It was almost like it subconsciously became second nature to us and before we knew it, we were participating in what we saw or we began speaking the language we heard.

As we watched the examples set before us, they began grooming our thoughts, words, and actions. Before we knew it, we knew what division and competition looked like. We even began whispering and fluently speaking the language of distasteful words with hopes that our opinions would provoke another broken Queens deepest insecurities to resurface.

Along the way, in some shape, form, or fashion, other hurt Queens began generating codes that taught many of us, if one Queen doesn't like the other, we must dislike them too and if we didn't abide by the code, we could no longer be friends. You know the saying, "You're fraternizing with the enemy." And this is why many Queens can't applaud one another publicly.

Queens, we didn't come out of the womb hating and speaking unkind words to or about each other. We were innocent, loving, and compassionate until someone with powerful influence came along and tainted us just as someone did them.

How do we expect things to change if we're unwilling to dethrone our pride and regenerate new codes that will reprogram each of our minds allowing us to see things through the eyes of God? Remember, *"Insanity is doing the same thing, over and over again, and expecting different results."* ~Albert Einstein

So, do we continue to negatively influence younger Queens who have the potential to impact millions of lives in a powerful way? Or do we leave behind a trail blaze of powerful Queens who will change the trajectory of the lives they encounter? My friend once said, *"Although we're imperfect and make mistakes, it's the corrective behavior and our come back in Christ that makes us stronger."*

It's time to come back Queens! We're better than what we've been taught. We can move forward in greatness and impact the lives of generations to come in such a way, that it will cause younger Queens to jump back in line and help rebuild others on a healthier foundation of love and forgiveness the way God intended. Ask yourself this, what version of the younger Queen would you like to see? You or a powerful Queen standing in her purpose? We must not neglect the fact that our younger Queens are in training and our actions and words are their trainer; therefore, we must remember it's not what we say, it how we say it. Our lives teach many lessons. So, we must be careful with the power of our influence by walking in obedience so that they too will follow.

Beautiful Outcomes
can happen if we simply make the necessary
Adjustments!

Prayer: Lord, guide my tongue that I may address things in love. Help me to respond with only gentle answers and kind words. (Proverbs 15:1) In Jesus name Amen!

CHAPTER SIX
It's Not What We Say; It's How We Say It

We live in a world where it's normal to say how we feel, but in such an unhealthy way that it invites chaos instead of peace. It's an unhealthy cycle that has become so popular, that it has dismantled moral principles given by God all for the sake of pride.

There's a saying that goes like this, "Girl, I'm gone tell it like it T—I— IS." The question is, who passed on this torch of dysfunction causing us to reach back, grab it, and run with unspeakable speed to win a race; only to later realize that the gold medal we won, was and is simply called deception.

Ephesians 4:26-27 says, *when you are angry, do not sin, and be sure to stop being angry before the end of the day. Do not give the devil a way to defeat you.* (NCV) But it's almost like we selfishly say, "I don't care how you feel as long as I've gotten how I feel off of my chest and I don't care how it makes you feel if I don't talk to you." Then, it becomes a domino effect that leaves behind broken families and broken friendships that many times leads to funerals and more prisons being filled with Queens who allowed anger to get the best of them.

Sadly, not many of us are stopping to think that something is seriously wrong with this. When will we get to a place where we no longer participate in passing on this torch that has been murdering spirits with this oh so powerful thing called our tongues that's locked, loaded, and ready to say just how we feel at any given moment?

We're beautiful Queens who have the power to break this cycle. So, we must intentionally think before we speak and make the necessary adjustments as to how we think about each other, to what we say to each other, how we say it, and our body language upon delivery in order to experience beautiful outcomes. There's beauty in our pain and hurt towards one another. She's hurting just like you and I. And if we all continue to sling hurt like stones, we'll be no better than the enemy who feeds on the lack of forgiveness and hate that we give each other. What do we really gain by satisfying our flesh (Our Wants Vs. Our Obedience to God) because the applauds eventually turn into whispers that question our integrity? Therefore, we must get to a place where we love one another in spite of what's been done or said to us or about us.

As a Queen deciding to be a part of the solution, I too must remember to love and forgive others who have hurt me in the past, who may hurt me now and, in the future. I'm not exempt from any of this. I'm on this journey with you and we urgently need to experience a more positive change.

We must stand in the truth that we are not b******, h***, or any other degrading names that have the ability to tilt or snatch our crowns. We must stand in the truth that, *"A gentle answer will calm a person's anger, but an unkind word will cause more anger."* (Proverbs 15:1)

Therefore, we must put down our knives (Harsh Words & Approach) and no longer cut down other Queens with our words leaving them in a puddle of blood to die. We must put down our shovels (Excuses & Justification) to bury our participation in hurting them and become accountable for what we too have done. We must put down the hammers (Gossip & Slander) that drives nails in other Queens hands and feet who are our sisters in Christ by remembering that Jesus didn't die for division because He's a God of unity.

We must be patient with the pain that other Queens are carrying and be a place of comfort for them. We must be accountable for our own actions and hurtful words that have caused many to commit suicide, give up on life, or even turn their backs on God who loves them so much.

Queens, we're all hurting. We all have shed many tears, but what we do have in common is, that we're Queens of God on the road to being healed. So, Queens, it's time to give her (whoever she may be) back her crown.

There is *Beauty* in our
Pain & Hurt
towards one another.

Prayer: Lord, help me to get to a place where I can love in spite of the pain and hurt that I've inflicted upon your daughters and to forgive them for the pain they have caused me. Please show me the beauty in all of this. In Jesus name Amen!

CHAPTER SEVEN
Lord, Are You Sure?

Have you ever hurt someone or has someone hurt you and you later hear those gut-wrenching words, "Go back and make it right?" I'm pretty sure we've all been there.

That's simply the sound of Heaven guiding us to rebuild what was once broken. Don't question it, but simply pray for God to soften the individual's hearts. Then, ask Him to set the date, give you the right words to say, and the ability to listen to understand and not just to respond. If we listen to respond, we'll miss crucial information that could lead to a relationship being restored.

Even if butterflies fill your stomach and curse words are ready to part your lips; wait because her truth is vital to this process. That's simply fear trying to detour you from hearing her truth and your purpose in forgiving her. *Mark 11:25* says, *when you are praying, if you are angry with someone, forgive him so that your Father in Heaven will also forgive you.* (NCV) Queens, in order for healing to take place, we must understand that healing isn't one sided. There are three sides; your side, her side, and The truth that God saw from all angles.

So, if what she says hurts; bite your tongue, hold your peace, pray, and simply be accountable for your part and forgive her for hers. To be honest, holding grudges isn't worth forfeiting the forgiveness that God wants to give us. I can hear my friend now saying, "Just because a person acts as if they don't care, doesn't mean that it doesn't hurt."

You see, many of us have been misled by the saying, "Out of site out of mind," until they see or hear about the individual, then, the pain resurfaces. This is why in moments of hurt, we must practice forgiveness immediately. Don't wait and let the pain fester, but cry it out and leave it with God. If not, that one moment of offense will begin infecting your spirit leaving you angry and bitter; therefore, causing you to ignore God as He softly whispers, "Go back and make it right!"

If you don't do it for you, please do it for the little Queens who are in training through the words and behavior they witness. We must be willing to swallow our pride and show them a new way because their fighting and killing one another, and their doing so in front of babies, young children, and other Queens who are desperately pleading for them to stop. They're clueless as to how their tainting young Queens with hate that has the potential to teach them how to deal with future disagreements. How devastating that must be for innocent children to have to witness such violence because unforgiveness has penetrated a hole in the hearts of those fighting one another.

We must be open to handling issues that others have with us with an open mind, even if the truth is painful to hear. We must be willing to break free from these unhealthy cycles of division in order to make the necessary adjustments to provoke change in our lives and the lives of those who are watching.

It's no longer a whisper behind her back or a giggle when she walks away. It's full blown physical fights with weapons and older Queens cosigning on the very thing that God hates—DIVISION. How many more Queens have to die or end up in prison before we break this cycle and make things right again? How long will we pass on this baton of dysfunction to the generations after us?

Actually Queens, How Did We Even Get Here?

When will we join hands and guide all Queens back together to pray and be the mediator of their pain instead of instigators causing more conflict? How long will it take for us to become one body unified in Christ to rebuild relationships that were once broken? It's time to stand up and be the example that our younger Queens need to see in order for them to finally pass on healthy solutions to dealing with disagreements and issues with one another. As iron sharpens iron, so people can improve each other. **(Proverbs 27:17)**

Just take a moment and really think about who you need to forgive. Even my heart breaks at the thought of the Queens that I haven't truly forgiven. Let's all get to a place where we can truly forgive and set those who have hurt us free even if they refuse to have that much needed conversation.

Queens, when God said love, forgive, encourage, and get along with one another; He meant that. His word doesn't change because we're mad with one another just to make us comfortable. He stands firm with what He's said. Forgive them for they know not what they do. (**Luke 23:34**) So, let's swallow our pride and silence the voices that instigate division, then obey the soft whisper of God saying, "Go back and make it right." Because He's sure about what He's asked us to do. Everyone else will eventually join the movement.

We must *boldly*
build a
Healthier Foundation of
Forgiveness

Prayer: Lord, I have mastered holding grudges against my fellow sisters in Christ, but I ask you to please help me to truly forgive them from my heart so that when I see them or hear their name, I will be at peace and love them with unconditional love. In Jesus name Amen!

CHAPTER EIGHT
Forgiveness

Have you ever refused to forgive someone with hopes that they would be manipulated by the emotional roller coaster the pain caused you, and give you the one thing you felt you deserved — an apology? Then, after it was all said and done, you realized that you were only hurting yourself. Well I have. Holding grudges robbed me of my peace and on that journey, I discovered that forgiveness was my key. But to what?

"To forgive is to set a prisoner free and discover that the prisoner was you." ~Louis B. Smedes

You may say, "But you don't understand, her words cut deep. There's no coming back from that." I get it and I'm sorry, but the pain left you with beautiful scars that tells the story of how you survived.

If we would just trust God, we'll see that forgiveness can restore any relationship. It's our unwillingness to do so that keeps us apart. The enemy doesn't want us to forgive one another, nor does he want Queens to be united in Christ because he knows that in that place would reside encouragement, prayer, and peace. That's why he constantly reminds us of what other Queens have done or said to us. If he can keep us divided, then we'll remain in a bitter and angry state of mind. Then, his job is done.

The sad part about this is that all it took was a whisper of deception from him that said, "Don't you remember when? She'll only do it again. Don't trust her. I'm telling you, you're gonna regret it." Then, he screams the biggest lie of them all, "SHE'S TOXIC!!!" (John 8:44) But what he forgot to tell you was this, *"Resentment is like drinking poison and then hoping it will kill your enemies."* ~Nelson Mandela

It's crazy because we believe the lies that he uses to instigate division and we many times ignore God. Even in the midst of our prideful disobedience, God continues to speak in His still small voice, *"Love covers a multitude of sin. Jesus didn't die for division. You must Forgive."*

Colossians 3:13 says, *"Get along with each other, and forgive each other. If someone does wrong to you, forgive that person because the Lord forgave you. Do all these things; but most important, love each other. Love is what holds you all together in perfect unity."*

We must search within and find the place where the hurt from our fellow Queens began so that God can begin healing each us. We must reflect over our lives and see what happened to the little Queens who used to play together and have fun. Don't you remember? We we're all united then and we couldn't wait to play as little kids do; and when we hurt one another, we quickly said, "I'm sorry. Can we be friends again?"

Who tainted the beauty of that friendship and taught us that it was okay to hate one another? Who instigated division and why? Where is the root of this dysfunctional thing called the double D's and I'm not talking about bras,

I'm talking about "Division and Discord?" **Proverbs 10:12** says it all, *"Hate stirs up strife, but love covers all offenses."*

So, we must boldly build a healthier foundation of forgiveness for the younger Queens watching before they become tainted with the unhealthy propagandas of unforgiveness as we were. Doing so will create a bridge for them to meet one another with the exact love and forgiveness that we have many times withheld from each other.

Sadly, at this very moment, the enemy is reconstructing more lies to keep us divided to taint the younger Queens who are watching so that they too can pass on this deceptive baton of pain to distract us from our purpose. That's why, we must be responsible with the power of our influence and show younger Queens what forgiveness looks like, what it feels like, and what it sounds like.

It's time to put down our carnal weapons of hate, pride, jealousy, gossip, fighting, lying, speaking ill of one another, and instigation that causes division. Then, we must pick up our spiritual weapons of empathy, love, truth, compassion, grace, mercy, patience, sympathy, accountability, and peace.

We must reevaluate our thoughts and hearts towards those who have hurt us because life is tough and we all need each other. Just look around at how unforgiveness has torn so many families and friendships apart. Can't you hear the cries of the parents who will never see their children again? Can't you hear the cries of mothers praying that their daughters survive and rededicate their lives to Christ while they're in prison? Just stop and listen. Queens, I can hear it. Do you?

So, now is the time to rebuild those broken relationships with Jesus on our side, but this time, with respect and love for one another. Lord knows we all need it. Remember, God is a God of unity and where His presence is, peaceful relationships can flourish. Love those who have hurt you, pray for the strength to forgive, and have the tough conversations as to where things went wrong and when it's all said and done, allow God time to repair what was once broken. And remember, *"To forgive is to set a prisoner free and discover that the prisoner was you."* ~Louis B. Smedes

Remind Her
Of her worth in
Christ!

Then, Give Her Back Her Crown

Prayer: Lord, please help me to remind myself and other Queens that they are am redeemed, forgiven, and worthy. Please help me to straighten their crowns; not tilt them. In Jesus name Amen!

CHAPTER NINE
Give Her Back Her Crown

As women, many of us carry mountains of pain on our backs and tons of heartbreaks in our hearts that influence us to respond out of character. In doing so, we tilt and snatch crowns leaving behind Queens that are broken beyond repair. Sadly, we've all experienced this but if you haven't, one day it will knock at your door as a beautifully wrapped gift waiting patiently for you to open it.

We've many times stepped outside of the will of God and left behind subliminal messages that have replaced encouragement and social media has become a nesting ground that holds so many women hostage to their past and present mistakes. It's sad because instead of magnifying and embracing their growth in Christ, we celebrate their fall and in those moments as she scrolls through her newsfeed, the embarrassment she's experienced introduces her to insecurities and regrets that consume her with thoughts and fears of never escaping the shame and the fear of never being worthy of wearing her crown again. Truthfully, I can only imagine how this breaks the heart of God to see how we've snatched away the confidence of others through our own brokenness.

Although it's a hard truth to accept, we many times lack spiritual discernment and assume that surely the Queen standing in front of us is the one we must attack by devaluing her with our words, subliminal messages, and our actions, but she's not. It's the enemy that invisibly uses her as a puppet on a string by manipulating her emotional state of mind as he whispers, "What she did is unforgiveable. Your forgiveness is too valuable for her." Can't you see him? I surely can! (Ephesians 6:12)

One day after making a choice I will forever regret, God lovingly opened my eyes and allowed me to see that we were groomed by others and our issues with one another to see another Queens darkness instead of her light that shines bright no matter how dim it may be. The truth is, even in the darkest places lights peeks through, we just have to be willing to see it. If we continue to tilt her crown by reminding her of her past and present mistakes or blindly seeing her through the blurred lens of who we assume her to be, we'll surely miss out on her shine in Christ. *Isaiah 43:18-19* says, *"Forget the things of the past, behold I do a knew thing. Don't you see it happening?"*

Just think about it. Do we really advance in life by tearing down one another? How does sharing videos of her most embarrassing moments or poor decisions help her recover from the shame that she's experienced or is experiencing? Does our hate for one another make us stronger in Christ or does it keep us divided? And what do we really gain from fighting one another or instigating and celebrating fights like untamed animals ready to devour someone as if they were our prey? Does it have purpose? Will it bring glory to God or our true enemy satan?

Romans 1:28-32 says, *"People did not think it was important to have a true knowledge of God. So, God left them and allowed them to have their own worthless thinking and to do things they should not do. They are filled with every kind of sin, evil, selfishness, and hatred. They are full of jealousy, murder, fighting, lying, and thinking the* worst about each other. They gossip and say evil things about each other. They hate God. They are rude and conceited and brag about themselves. They invent ways of doing evil. They do not obey their parents. They are foolish, they do not keep their promises, and they show no kindness or mercy to others. They know God's law says that those who live like this should die. But they themselves not only continue to do these evil things; **_they applaud others who do them_**."

I think that we've all missed the big picture here, and that is that we all share similar stories and pains that we can encourage each other through, yet we fight one another and jealousy plagues us as we slander each other's name.

So, what do we really gain from snatching another Queens crown and why is it so hard to celebrate one another? God birthed us all into this world with purpose. A purpose that will bring Him glory. A purpose that will cause each of us to grow together in Christ. A purpose that will cause light to shine in someone else's darkness. A purpose that will cause broken Queens to meet at that once burnt bridge and rebuild it together so that we'll be able to walk across it to straighten the crowns we've titled and to pick up the crowns we've knocked down along the way and unite as one body; not as divided Queens ready to be slaughtered in battle by the enemy.

We're more than conquerors and we must stand in that knowing that our purpose is yearning to be set free. Our past only leaves behind lessons and wisdom to pass on to others so they won't continue to make the same mistakes we've made. You see, God knows the end of her story and we won't find it in her past.

Young Queens are depending on us to heal from our pain and issues with one another because they're in need of a new and healthier way to deal with their future issues because the way we've been doing it aint working.

The truth is, that bridge never burned down because God's extinguisher put the fire out before it was damaged beyond repair. It's our pride and inability to forgive that caused us to unwillingly go back, straighten, or give her back the crown that we titled or snatched and begin repairing what we assumed was destroyed. So, do we choose to go back and replace the damaged wood or continue to set fire to what God's grace and mercy extinguished. It's time to give her back her crown.

In God's eyes, we're no better than the next Queen. We must encourage one another and remind each other that we can make it through anything. How else would we be able to remind her that she can get back up and start again if we never knew what it felt like to fall? God allowed that door to open to show us that forgiveness was our key to unlock the door that we thought would never open again. I can see broken Queens kneeled down in tears as the Queen who hurt her straightens her crown in the presence of God. I can see broken Queens praising God as the Queen who hurt her gives her the crown that she assumed she would never be worthy enough to wear again.

Queen, can't you see it. We're better than this. We're better than the hurt. We're better than the pain. Don't allow her to leave this earth full of pain because that friendship was never restored. Please don't let her enter the grave without restoring the relationship that the enemy told you wasn't worthy of being restored again. Queens, can you hear me? Can you feel my pain? Can you see the tears that fall from my face as I type this? Close your eyes and allow yourself to feel see and again. God has blessings stored up for each of us, but what if it's our own filthy hands, words, and actions that's hindering us from receiving them? Therefore, we must lift up our heads and get back into our position of worthiness. We must get back into our position of peace and strength, so that we'll no longer allow the reminders of our past or shame to consume us and cause us to lower our heads again. God is leading us from those dark places just as He has done for others.

So, we must treat each other with love and respect. We must remind other Queens of their worthy and no longer allow our issues with one another to mold us. Instead of gossiping and laughing at what another Queen goes through, we must encourage her and remind her that she's still loved by God. We must remember that no matter what we've been through, we can still bounce back and stand in the fact that God still calls us worthy. For He knows the plans that He has for us. They are plans to give us hope and a good future. (Jeremiah 29:11) Remember, we are a Queens and when our past or present life tries to tilt or snatch our crown; we must square our shoulders back, stare them in their eyes, and say with respect, class, and confidence in Christ,

"Give Me Back My Crown!"

Love
Can Unlock Things
That Hate Tries to Hold Hostage!

.

Prayer: Lord, please help me to stand in love and be an example for the Queens watching. Help me to remember that this walk is for You to get all glory. In Jesus name Amen!

CHAPTER TEN
It's Bigger Than Us

You know, it's funny how we go through things with the assumption that the pain, embarrassment, and shame are about us. It's crazy how we miss the message until it comes back full circle. Then, we realize that it was always bigger than us. In the midst of all that we've been through and what we're going through now, are solutions and answers for someone else. And as we endure the trials we experience, our ability to be selfless will leave behind keys for them to escape.

Right now, millions of young Queens are in dire need of better solutions. Solutions that will cause generations to come to prosper beyond measure. Our foundation will be so strong in Christ, that we'll be able to rescue Queens who are being held hostage by hate and unforgiveness. And guess what? Our love and acceptance will be the keys that will set them free. Our unity will be so powerful that not even hate will be able to penetrate it. That's why we must urgently unite as one in Christ. In Him we will experience healing, peace, reconciliation, and a place where broken Queens are put back together again.

The truth is, we've all hurt each other in some kind of way, but we must be willing to maturely accept our part so that we'll be able to extend love and forgiveness to those who have hurt us. There's no more blaming Eve for what's going on in the world today because **Romans 2:15** confirms that we all have consciences that tell us when we're doing right and when we're doing wrong. It's our inability to move forward in love that hinders our growth.

In spite of it all, this walk that we're on has purpose and Eve stood in hers. If we continue to choose to eat from the bitter plate of her mistakes instead of the sweet taste from the dessert of her wisdom, we'll miss the point of her fall. Reality is, that her conversation with the enemy who deceitfully slithered in on the belly of a snake left behind the explanations to her curiosity and disobedience.

So, we must give her back her crown and get to a place where we truly honor God's word by getting along with each other instead of walking in the shoes of Cain, killing God's treasured Queens and attempting to hide their remains. As she cradles her pillow or falls down to her knees in prayer, her tears begin to scream. Just listen! Can't you hear her broken spirit? It has the same sound as Abel's did when his blood cried out from the rocks. Queens, our pain never fell on deaf ears. God heard everything. Even our emotions that didn't have the ability to form words for us to pray.

That's why we must intentionally be examples of love, patience, forgiveness, unity, and a healthy resolve because if not, the generations after us will be a slaughter house where Queens are mentally, physically, spiritually, and emotionally slaughtered or traumatized. And guess what? We wouldn't want to pay respects to that burial ground because we too will leave broken. We'll leave broken because we missed the bigger picture of their pain and the true meaning of the love and forgiveness that we've been withholding from one another.

Love is not easily angered, it always hopes, always trusts, and rejoices in truth. It doesn't boast, it's not proud, and it doesn't count up wrongs. It's patient, it always protects, and it doesn't delight in evil. Queens, love is so powerful that it doesn't dishonor others and it perseveres through all things. It's not self-seeking nor does it speak the language of envy. Love will never fail.

Since this is the case, why do we think that we're better than others when we're all equal in the sight of God? Why do we hate one another? Why do we lose hope in relationships being restored? Why do we forget that the pain caused by others is in God's control and that He has the power to heal it? Queens, we're all crucial pieces of a picture-perfect puzzle of diverse and unified Queens standing strong in Christ ready to battle with unconditional love.

So, why can't we attentively listen as she articulates how she feels without ignoring the fact that we contributed to her pain then, extend a sincere apology? Why do we stubbornly withhold forgiveness? Why do we remind each other of things of the past that we have the ability to resolve? Why do we give up on other Queens when they allow their pain to cry out the only way they know how?

Why not use our words to build and refuse to slander another Queens name? Why grow weary in doing good when we can stand together as one in Christ? Why drink the poison of jealousy, selfishly think of ourselves, and continue to fail the present and future Queens with division; instead of leading them to unity? Remember, love is the key that will unlock things that hate has held hostage in our hearts for far too long. It's time to rise up and remember that Love Always Wins!

Queens remember, it's bigger than me. It's bigger than you. It's bigger than us.

God Birthed
you into this world with purpose.
A *Purpose* that still sits within
Waiting to break free.

Prayer: Lord, I know that I was born with an assignment from You, but sometimes I lose focus of my purpose. Please help me to stay focused on the mission You have assigned me to do. And if I get distracted and forget what it is, please gently remind me of what I'm supposed to be doing. In Jesus name Amen!

CHAPTER TWELVE
Carry Her

With so many wounded Queens in the world losing hope, committing suicide, turning to drugs and alcohol, our hearts should be broken. We must choose to pick them up and carry them through their pain. We must be patient and love them even when they lash out because they're simply broken and in need of other Queens of God to carry them in prayer and encouraging words that will build them; not break them.

Sadly, while other Queens bash her name causing her to carry a heavy weight of shame and a broken spirit, they have no clue to the fact that she's crying out to God to deliver her from what she's going through. With no shoulder to cry on and no one to confide in; she breaks down from the heavy weights that we call life. This is the story of many Queens who are in need of help. I'm reminded of the scripture of the paralyzed man whose friends carried him to the place of Jesus and lowered him through the hole of the building.

They saw his need and made no excuse to get him to where he needed to be. They knew that there would be challenges along the way, but they chose to carry him anyway. They knew that on the other side of those challenges, was healing and hope for a friend. They weren't concerned about how long it would take, what people would think, or how far they had to go because their love would give them the strength they needed to carry him to the place that Jesus awaited his presence.

How wonderful it would be if we carried each other instead of shaming, degrading, and devaluing one another? How wonderful would it be to see other Queens healed and whole in spite of how long it took? How wonderful it would be to silence the gossip that's causing other Queens to lower their heads in shame? How wonderful it would be to help restore the relationships that broke her? How wonderful it would be to see the generations after us stand in unity instead of division?

Queens, there's beauty in her pain. God never told us to walk away, our flesh guided us. Remember, *the spirit is willing, but the flesh is weak.* (Matthew 26:41) Reality is, we all have so much in common. More than we will ever know and until we tap into that truth, we will continue this unhealthy cycle called division.

There were times in my life when I was a part of the problem until God softly whispered to me, "Where is the unity amongst my Queens?" That whisper quickly and lovingly checked me. So, as I write these words, believe me, they're also for me.

Queens are hurting and we must get to a place where we no longer justify our reasons to gossip, devalue, and hate one another to a place of understanding and valuing the healing that can happen from each of our pains. Our differences make up what we need to complete the puzzle of unity and love is our glue. We must love her unconditionally in spite of anything she's done. We must present be patient with her and understand that it may take time for her to heal. And in our moments of waiting, we must carry her in prayer, shower her with encouraging words, and lovingly redirect her.

God didn't look at that Queen and say, "She's no longer worthy." He didn't arrogantly lift His nose in the air or turn His back on her. He waited and still waits for her patiently. Ask yourself this question, *what if God decided to close his eyes, cover His ears, and turn His back on us during the roughest times in our lives or because we decided to drop His Queen due to us feeling that she was too unworthy of our attention to her pain?*

Honestly, we wouldn't want to know how that feels. I know I wouldn't! So, Queens, although it may be tough; carry her. Although she may have hurt you; carry her. Although her words and actions may have left you in a puddle of blood to die; carry her because on the other side of your strength to forgive, encourage, and carry her is your blessing. But don't just do it for the blessing. Do it because she's worthy of being loved and carried.

Remember, younger Queens are in training and as they watch us, they will either learn how to carry or drop the Queens they encounter. I know this will take some time to adjust to but, we can do all things through Christ who give us strength. We must choose to become a part of the solution because the problem/problems have caused too many women to suffer unjustly at the hands of other Queens.

We must no longer allow others to pass on unhealthy batons for us to reach back and finish the race that will later dethrone us to the lowest place in our lives needing someone to carry us.

Remember, love covers a multitude of sin and its love that will carry her. It's forgiveness that will carry her. It's genuine prayers and patience that will carry her. It's the choice to become a part of the solution that will give her back her crown that her pain, her past, the devil's deception, and the world took from her.

As we carry her, we will learn that her pain was her testimony and our ability and choice to carry her allowed her to reach the Queens blooming in her garden; to save them from what she went through with the wisdom she uses to water them.

Queens young and old, I now pass on a healthy baton of wisdom for you to carry and win the race. On your mark, get set, GO!

Recover
So That Someone Else Can Heal

Prayer: Lord, please heal me so that I can help someone else who may be experiencing what I'm going through. In Jesus name I pray Amen!

CHAPTER THIRTEEN
You Can Recover

We've all experienced pain, embarrassment, and rejection that we thought we'd never recover from, but you can, and your choice to do so will influence another Queen to do the same. Therefore, I want to take a moment to pour into every Queen young or old that has dropped out of school, every daughter with an absent mother, and every Queen who has fallen to drugs and alcohol to numb her pain. Although it hurts. It will work for your good.

So, to every high school dropout who feels like she will never succeed; my Queen, you can still earn your GED. Colleges all over the world accepts them because they see the value in your fall. Nothing has changed, but your perspectives. God never gave up on you. So, don't you dare give up on yourself. Even if you're your own cheerleader, cheer like your life depends on it. As you dust yourself off and put back on your crown, remember, you can do all things through Christ who gives you strengthen.

To every young girl, teenager, and adult whose mother was not present in your life, get back up. It's time to throw away the glasses that distorted your vision and see your mother's choices with new perspectives. I can only imagine how bad it hurts to have a living mother and no relationship with her, but I do know what it's like to not have a mother on earth at all. It's a pain and loneliness that I have no words to describe. I had to change my perspectives to clearly see the purpose of her absence. I had to recover from the pain that tortured me and stole my joy, and so can you.

Maybe, just maybe your mother had to let you go in order for you to break the curse. Maybe she needed for you to succeed where she failed. Maybe she needs for you to heal so that you can come back and rescue her. Yes, it may hurt and you may care less about her at this moment in your life, but what if she only passed on to you what was passed on to her? What if fear gripped her as the enemy told her that she was unfit to be your mother? What if she never healed from her own pain? I know you may feel that her choice was selfish, but love her anyway. Because if not, you'll find yourself repeating the same cycle that hurt you. So, bounce back Queen and recover because your pain has purpose.

To those who have fallen to drugs and alcohol, you no longer have to hide due to shame. You can fully recover from this because Queen, you have purpose. Nothing has changed because you are still worthy in the eyes of God and no one can change His mind about that. So, get back up and walk in your purpose. You're not what people have called you. You're not the pain that happened to you. You're not the lies that the enemy softly whispered in your ears so that no one else could hear him to combat his lies with the truth. You're more than a conqueror. You are redeemed and you have purpose.

I can only imagine the pain that you've been through, but Queen, there's no pain that God can't heal. I apologize on behalf of everyone who laughed as you coped the only way you knew how causing you to run to the very thing that was killing you. Today, I give you back your crown.

And to the rest of my fellow Queens, you too can recover from whatever you're going through. Even if there's no one there to help you; get up. Even if you have to crawl to the closest thing to regain your footing, start crawling, but don't you dare lay there and die. God has work for you to do.

We must **Honor** *the Prayers of the Queens before us through our obedience to God.*

Prayer: Lord, please forgive us for dishonoring our mothers and the Queens before us. Help us to respect, honor, and love them as You have commanded us. In Jesus name Amen

The Vow

To the Mothers who worked hard to raise us to have dignity, respect, and to honor God with our lives, we ask you to find it in your hearts to forgive us for mishandling the wisdom of love that you imparted into us. Your ability to convey such a message was simply for us to grow and be better than the generations before us.

Forgive us for our stubborn and disrespectful ways, as well as our unkind words and actions that many times caused you pain. Forgive us for our failure to acknowledge and understand that you could only parent us with the wisdom and knowledge that was passed on to you. Forgive us for fighting one another when you encouraged us to forgive and please forgive us for passing on such arrogance and pride to those after us because we assumed we knew it all.

Our actions simply displayed how ignorant, immature, and rebellious we were and, in some cases, still are. We now see that your fight was productive because you won your battles spiritually in fasting and prayer; not physically. And because of this, many saw the love of Christ that shined brightly through you.

We thank you for standing firm in prayer when we rebelled against the wisdom you gained from your mistakes. Thank you for talking even when we didn't want to listen and thank you for your patience in not giving up on us.

From this day forward, we vow to respond with gentleness and love instead of hate. We vow to fight each of our battles in prayer instead of physically, through revenge, and with unkind words. We vow to no longer rebel against God and to become one in Christ as He intended.

And to the mothers who now watch over us; it breaks our hearts that we didn't operate in love, forgiveness, patience, and kindness towards you. We will never be able to go back and make our wrongs right because you can't answer us from the grave. Your ears can no longer hear and your heart no longer pumps the blood that will give you the opportunity to forgive us.

We deeply regret how we hurt you. We must now move forward in Christ by vowing to build and not break; love and not hate, to forgive and no longer hold grudges. We vow to respect our elders and one another so that we can truly experience God's peace. We vow to put on our spiritual battle gear and fight our true enemy, satan. We vow to be better Queens.

Queens!!!

As we heal from our deepest pains towards one another, we will find that our journeys were never about us. Our journeys were simply examples for the Younger Queens that were quietly watching.

We must learn from our mistakes & show them a better way before it's too late because there's a younger generation quietly watching them.

So, let's begin the process of returning snatched crowns & straightening the one's that have been tilted to silence the whispers that have made them feel unworthy.

The Whispers

Many go through trials quiet & alone
Their transparency is too much to handle
And deemed as negative energy.
The dark comforts them
& as their fellow Christians walks away,

It whispers,

"Didn't I tell you that no one cares?
To them you're only a sinner.
Don't worry, I'll cradle you in my arms
& smile as I wipe away your tears.
No one wants to hear your drama.
They can't take away your pain.
They'll watch as you fall & laugh in your face!"

She shakes herself & cries out for help!

Finally, prayer warriors stepped in
With encouragement that brought relief as
Peace held her tightly and whispered,

"God loves you so much! He understands your pain!
His presence is all around you!
Even when you feel alone & like you were going insane.
When you cry, Jesus intercedes!

Because He too understands!
He felt it on the cross & even in the wilderness!
I know that your silence screamed,

FATHER WHY HAVE YOU FORSAKEN ME!

Just as Jesus did!
And just like Jesus, that's NOT how your story will end!
Your scars tell the story of the pain you've felt!
As loneliness rumbled like thunder
And darkness attempted to hide your light!

It could not withstand the scars of Jesus
& His Blood that flowed to your once dry river
That was filled with rocks of sadness
And dust from shame
That tried to cover your tears
As you transparently told a story
That many refused to hear!

But even when their ears rejected you
My blood accepted you and washed you clean!
The holes in my hand made room
For your ugly pain to slide through.
My job was never to walk away
But to see that you made it through in peace

Not PIECES!!!

My goal is NEVER to break your spirit
But to build you up for me to get ALL Glory!!!!
Now SPEAK to help someone else
Make it through the same storms
That tried to kill you!

When I ascended
I left the Holy Spirit as your comforter!
So, here I am to wrap you in my LOVE!!!"

Prayer of Forgiveness

Father God, forgive me for the crowns that I have tilted and snatched through my own pain. Forgive me for my failure to forgive when Your daughters hurt me. Forgive me for not being obedient when You told me to make it right. Forgive me for causing Your Queens to become insecure. Forgive me for every Queen that I hurt to the point of driving her to drugs and alcohol to numb her of the pain. Forgive me for causing others to walk away from You because I refused to line up with Your word. Forgive me for not being mindful of how I communicated my frustrations. Lord please forgive me for not listening to understand. Teach me Lord how to build Your Queens; instead of tearing them down. Help me to truly listen and understand before I speak. Help me to set better examples for the younger Queens who are quietly watching me. And Lord please forgive me for **All** known and unknown sins in Your Son Jesus name Amen!

Romans 15:1-7

"We who are strong in faith should help the weak with their weaknesses, and not please only ourselves. Let each of us please our neighbors for their good, to help them be stronger in faith. Even Christ did not live to please himself. It was as the Scriptures said: "When people insult you, it hurts me." Everything that was written in the past was written to teach us. The Scriptures give us patience and encouragement so that we can have hope.

May the patience and encouragement that come from God allow you to live in harmony with each other the way Christ Jesus wants. Then you will all be joined together, and you will give glory to God the Father of our Lord Jesus Christ. Christ accepted you, so you should accept each other, which will bring glory to God."

Let's Rebuild Broken Queens

Our pain always tells a beautiful story even as we go through trials and tribulations. Our pain is never wasted because it fertilizes our future. Even when our faith goes from big to small, God reminds us of our faith that's the size of a mustard seed. We must pray for our sisters even when we don't understand what they're going through. Our ways are not His ways and His thoughts are not our thoughts. We must acknowledge Him and He will direct our oaths. God is always guiding us to comfort one another and to intercede with loving prayers.

If you haven't already accepted the gift of eternal life through Jesus; it's still available. Simply say, "Lord, forgive me for allowing my pain to push me away from You. I accept Jesus as my Lord and Savior because He died and rose for me. In Jesus name Amen."

Scripture References

Isaiah 61:3 I will give them a crown to replace their ashes, and oil of gladness to replace their sorrow, and clothes of praise to replace their broken spirit of sadness. Then, they will be called trees planted by the Lord to show His greatness. (NCV)

Matthew 18:15-17 If your fellow believer sins against you, go and tell him in private what he did wrong. If he listens to you, you have helped that person to be your brother or sister again. But if he refuses to listen, go to him again and take one or two other people with you. 'Every case may be proved by two or three witnesses.' If he refuses to listen to them, tell the church. If he refuses to listen to the church, then treat him like a person who does not believe in God or like a tax collector. (NCV)

Ephesians 4:26-27 When you are angry, do not sin, and be sure to stop being angry before the end of the day. Do not give the devil a way to defeat you. (NCV)

Matthew 11:25 When you are praying, if you are angry with someone, forgive him so that your Father in Heaven will also forgive you. (NCV)

Ephesians 6:12 Our fight is not against people on earth but against the rulers and authorities and the powers of this world's darkness, against the spiritual powers of evil in the heavenly world. (NCV)

Isaiah 43:18-19 Forget the things of the past, behold I do a knew thing. Don't you see it happening? (NCV)

Romans 1:28-32 People did not think it was important to have a true knowledge of God. So, God left them and allowed them to have their own worthless thinking and to do things they should not do. They are filled with every kind of sin, evil, selfishness, and hatred. They are full of jealousy, murder, fighting, lying, and thinking the worst about each other. They gossip and say evil things about each other. They hate God. They are rude and conceited and brag about themselves. They invent ways of doing evil. They do not obey their parents. They are foolish, they do not keep their promises, and they show no kindness or mercy to others. They know God's law says that those who live like this should die. But they themselves not only continue to do these evil things; they applaud others who do them. (NCV)

Colossians 3:13 Get along with each other, and forgive each other. If someone does wrong to you, forgive that person because the Lord forgave you. Do all these things; but most important, love each other. Love is what holds you all together in perfect unity. (NCV)

Proverbs 10:12 Hate stirs up strife, but love covers all offenses. (NCV)

Romans 8:26 Also, the Spirit helps us with our weakness. We do not know how to pray as we should. But the Spirit himself speaks to God for us, even begs God for us with deep feelings that words cannot explain. (NCV)

Psalm 56:8 You have recorded my troubles. You have kept a list of my tears. Aren't they in your records? (NCV)

Mark 11:25 When you are praying, if you are angry with someone, forgive him so that your Father in heaven will also forgive your sins. (NCV)

Luke 23:34 Jesus said, "Father, forgive them, because they don't know what they are doing." (NCV)

John 8:44 You belong to your father the devil, and you want to do what he wants. He was a murderer from the beginning and was against the truth, because there is no truth in him. When he tells a lie, he shows what he is really like, because he is a liar and the father of lies. (NCV)

Proverbs 15:1 A gentle answer will calm a person's anger, but an unkind answer will cause more anger. (NCV)

Proverbs 27:17 As iron sharpens iron, so people can improve each other. (NCV)

Jeremiah 29:11 I say this because I know what I am planning for you," says the Lord. "I have good plans for you, not plans to hurt you. I will give you hope and a good future. (NCV)

Matthew 26:41 Stay awake and pray for strength against temptation. The spirit wants to do what is right, but the body is weak." (NCV)

Quote References

"Our deepest fear is not that we are inadequate. Our deepest fear is that we are powerful beyond measure. It is our light, not our darkness that most frightens us. We ask ourselves, 'Who am I to be brilliant, gorgeous, talented, or fabulous?' Actually, who are you not to be? You are a child of God." ~**Marianne Williamson**

"I hold that a strongly marked personality can influence descendants for generations." ~**Beatrix Potter**

"Insanity is doing the same thing, over and over again, and expecting different results." ~**Albert Einstein**

"To forgive is to set a prisoner free and discover that the prisoner was you." ~**Louis B. Smedes**

"Resentment is like drinking poison and then hoping it will kill your enemies." ~**Nelson Mandela**

About the Author

I am a mother, advocate, wife, and the CEO of Ginyard Publishing. I am also the screenwriter, producer & director of No Perfect Love which will be coming Soon. I enjoy writing & creating new ways to share the gift that God has given me with the world by standing in my purpose. Although I enjoy writing & creating, it doesn't define me. I'm simply an **Imperfect** Queen created by God. Learn more at www.IamLakisha.com

Stay Connected:
Instagram: @IamLakishaL @NoPerfectLoveMovie

Facebook: @iamlakisha @NoPerfectLoveMovie @ginyardpublishing

Give
Her Back Her
CROWN

& Empower other women to do the same.

Made in the USA
Columbia, SC
02 November 2020

23857329R00071